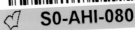

MEMORIES LOOK AT ME

ALSO BY TOMAS TRANSTRÖMER
FROM NEW DIRECTIONS

The Great Enigma: New Collected Poems

Tomas Tranströmer

Memories Look at Me

A Memoir

Translated from the Swedish by Robin Fulton

 A NEW DIRECTIONS BOOK

First published in Sweden as *Minnena ser mig* in 1993 by Bonnierförlagen AB, Box 3159,
103 63 Stockholm.
Published by arrangement with Bloodaxe Books Ltd., Highgreen, Tarset, Northum-
berland, NE48 1RP, UK.

Manufactured in the United States of America.
New Directions Books are printed on acid-free paper.
First published in *The Great Enigma: New Collected Poems* (NDP1050) in 2006 and as a New
Directions Paperbook (NDP1229) in 2011.
Published simultaneously in Canada by Penguin Books Canada Limited.
Design by Erik Rieselbach

Library of Congress Cataloging-in-Publication Data

Tranströmer, Tomas, 1931–
[Minnena ser mig. English]
Memories look at me : a memoir / Tomas Transtromer ; translated from the Swedish
by Robin Fulton.
p. cm.
"A New Directions book."
Includes bibliographical references and index.
ISBN 978-0-8112-2018-7 (pbk. : alk. paper)
1. Tranströmer, Tomas, 1931– 2. Authors, Swedish—20th century—Biography.
I. Fulton, Robin. II. Title.
PT9876.3.R3Z4713 2011
839.73′74—dc23
[B]

2011043110

10 9 8 7 6 5 4 3 2 1

New Directions Books are published for James Laughlin
by New Directions Publishing Corporation
80 Eighth Avenue, New York, NY 10011

MEMORIES LOOK AT ME

Memories

"My life." Thinking these words, I see before me a streak of light. On closer inspection it has the form of a comet. The brightest end, the head, is childhood and growing up. The nucleus, the densest part, is infancy, that first period, in which the most important features of our life are determined. I try to remember, I try to penetrate that density. But it is difficult to move in these concentrated regions, it is dangerous, it feels as if I am coming close to death itself. Further back, the comet thins out—that's the longer part, the tail. It becomes more and more sparse, but also broader. I am now far out in the comet's tail, I am sixty as I write this.

Our earliest experiences are for the most part inaccessible. Retellings, memories of memories, reconstructions based on moods that suddenly flare into life.

My earliest datable memory is a feeling. A feeling of pride. I have just turned three and it has been declared that this is very significant, that I am now big. I'm in bed in a bright room, then clamber down to the floor stunningly aware of the fact that I am becoming a grown-up. I have a doll to whom I gave the most beautiful name I could think of: Karin Spinna. I don't treat her in a motherly fashion. She is more like a comrade or someone I am in love with.

We live in Stockholm, in the Söder area, at Swedenborgsgatan 33 (now called Grindsgatan). Father is still part of the family but is soon to leave. Our ways are quite "modern"—right from the start I use the familiar *du* form with my parents. My mother's parents are close by, just around the corner, in Blekingegatan.

My maternal grandfather, Carl Helmer Westerberg, was born in 1860. He was a ship's pilot and a very good friend of mine, seventy-one years older than myself. Oddly enough, the same difference in age existed between him and his own maternal grandfather, who was born in 1789: the storming of the Bastille, the Anjala mutiny, Mozart writing his Clarinet Quintet. Two equal steps back in time, two long steps, yet not really so very long. We can touch history.

Grandfather's way of speech belonged to the nineteenth century. Many of his expressions would seem surprisingly old-fashioned today. But in his mouth, and to my ear, they felt altogether natural. He was a fairly short man, with a white moustache and a prominent and rather crooked nose—"like a Turk's," as he said. His temperament was lively and he could flare up at any moment. His occasional outbursts were never taken too seriously and they were over as soon as they had begun. He was quite without persistent aggression. Indeed he was so conciliatory that he risked being labeled as soft. He wanted to keep on the best side even of people who might be criticized—in their absence—in the course of ordinary conversation. "But surely you must agree that X is a crook!" "Well, well— that's something I don't really know about…."

After the divorce, Mother and I moved to Folkunga-gatan 57, a lower-middle-class tenement, where a motley crowd lived in close proximity to one another. My memories of life in that tenement arrange themselves like scenes from a film of the thirties or forties, with the appropriate list of characters. The lovable concierge, her strong laconic husband whom I admired because, among other things, he had been poisoned by gas, which suggested a heroic closeness to dangerous machines.

A steady trickle of comers and goers didn't belong there. The occasional drunk would slowly return to his wits on the stairway. Several times a week beggars would ring. They would stand on the porch mumbling. Mother made sandwiches for them—she gave them slices of bread rather than money.

We lived on the fifth floor. At the top, that is. There were four doors, plus the entry to the attic. On one of them was the name Orke, press photographer. In a way it seemed grand to live beside a press photographer.

Our next-door neighbor was a bachelor, well into middle age, yellowish complexion. He worked at home, running some sort of broker's business by phone. In the course of his calls he often gave vent to hilarious guffaws that burst through the walls into our apartment. Another recurring sound was the pop of corks. Beer bottles didn't have metal caps then. Those Dionysiac sounds, the guffaws of laughter and the popping of corks, seemed hardly to belong to the spectrally pale old fellow we sometimes met in the elevator. As the years passed he became suspicious and the bouts of laughter diminished in frequency.

Once, there was an outbreak of violence. I was quite small. A neighbor had been locked out by his wife; he was drunk and furious and she had barricaded herself in. He tried to break down the door and bawled out various threats. I remember him screaming the peculiar sentence: "I don't give a damn if I go to Kungsholmen!" I asked Mother what he meant, about Kungsholmen. She explained that the police headquarters was there. From then on that part of town evoked a sense of something fearful. (This feeling intensified when I visited St. Erik's Hospital and saw the war-wounded from Finland being cared for in the winter of 1939–40.)

Mother left for work early in the morning. She didn't take a tram or bus—throughout her entire adult life she walked from Söder to Östermalm, Östermalm to Söder. She worked in the Hedvig Leonora School and was in charge of the third and fourth grades year after year. She was a devoted teacher, deeply involved with the children. One might imagine it would be hard for her to accept retirement. But it wasn't—she felt greatly relieved.

Since Mother worked we had home-help, a "maid" as she was called, though "child-minder" would have been nearer the truth. She slept in a tiny room that was really part of the kitchen and which was not included in the official apartment-with-two-rooms-and-kitchen designation of our home.

When I was five or six, our maid was called Anna-Lisa and she came from Eslöv, in Skåne, in the south of Sweden. I thought she was very attractive: frizzy blond hair, a turned-up nose, a mild Skåne accent. She was a lovely person and I still feel something special when I pass Eslöv station. But I have never actually stepped off the train at that magic place.

Anna-Lisa was particularly talented at drawing. Disney figures were her specialty. I myself drew almost uninterruptedly throughout those years, in the late 1930s. Grandfather brought home rolls of brown paper of the sort then used in all the grocery shops, and I filled the sheets with illustrated stories. I had, to be sure, taught myself to write at the age of five. But it was too slow a process. My imagination needed some speedier means of expression. I didn't even have enough patience to draw properly. I developed a kind of shorthand sketching method with figures in violent movement: breakneck drama yet no details. Cartoon strips consumed only by myself.

One day in the mid-1930s I disappeared in the middle of Stockholm. Mother and I had been to a school concert. In the crush by the exit I lost my grasp of her hand. I was carried helplessly away by the human current, and since I was so small I could not be discovered. Darkness was falling over Hötorget. I stood at the exit, robbed of all sense of security. There were people around me but they were intent on their own business. There was nothing to hold on to. It was my first experience of death.

After an initial period of panic I began to think. It should be possible to walk home. It was absolutely possible. We had come by bus. I had knelt on the seat as I usually did and looked out of the window. Drottninggatan had flowed past. What I had to do now, simply, was to walk back the same way, bus stop by bus stop.

I went in the right direction. Of that long walk I have a clear memory of only one part—of reaching Norrbro and seeing the water under the bridge. The traffic here was heavy and I didn't dare set off across the street. I turned to a man who was standing beside me and said: "There's a lot of traffic here." He took me by the hand and led me across.

But then he let go of me. I don't know why this man and all the other unknown adults thought it was quite alright for a little boy to wander by himself through

Stockholm on a dark evening. But that's how it was. The remainder of the journey—through Gamla Stan, the old town, over Slussen and into Söder—must have been complicated. Perhaps I homed in on my destination with the help of the same mysterious compass that dogs and carrier pigeons have in them—no matter where they are released they always find their way home. I remember nothing of this part of my journey. Well, yes, I do—I remember how my self-confidence grew and grew, so that when I did at last arrive home I was euphoric. Grandfather met me. My devastated mother was sitting in the police station following the progress of their search for me. Grandfather's firm nerves didn't fail him; he received me quite naturally. He was relieved of course, but didn't make a fuss. It all felt secure and natural.

Museums

As a child I was attracted to museums. First, the Natural History Museum. What a building! Gigantic, Babylonian, inexhaustible! On the ground floor, hall after hall of stuffed mammals and birds thronged in the dust. And the arches, smelling of bones, where the whales hung from the roof. Then one floor up: the fossils, the invertebrates …

I was taken to the Natural History Museum when I was only about five years old. At the entrance, two elephant skeletons met the visitor. They were the two guardians of the gateway to the miraculous. They made an overwhelming impression on me and I drew them in a big sketchbook.

After a time, those visits to the Natural History Museum stopped. I started to go through a phase of being quite terrified of skeletons. The worst was the bony figure depicted at the end of the article on "Man" in the *Nordic Family Lexicon*. But my fear was aroused by skeletons in general, including the elephant skeletons at the entrance to the museum. I became frightened even of my own drawing of them and couldn't bring myself to open the sketchbook.

My interest turned to the Railway Museum. Nowadays it occupies spacious premises just outside the town of Gävle, but back then the entire museum was squeezed into a part of the district of Klara right in the center of Stockholm. Twice a week Grandfather and I made our way down from Söder and visited the museum. Grandfather himself must have been enthralled by the model trains, otherwise he would hardly have endured so many visits. When we decided to make a day of it we would finish up in Stockholm Central Station, which was nearby, and watch the trains come steaming in, life-sized.

The museum staff noticed the zeal of the young boy, and on one occasion I was taken into the museum office and allowed to write my name (with a back-to-front S) in a visitors' book. I wanted to be a railway engineer. I was, however, more interested in steam engines than in electric ones. In other words, I was more romantic than technical.

Some time later, as a schoolboy, I returned to the Natural History Museum. I was now an amateur zoologist, solemn, like a little professor. I sat bent over books about insects and fish.

I had started my own collections. They were kept at home in a cupboard. But inside my skull grew an immense museum and a kind of interplay developed between this imaginary one and the very real one that I visited.

I visited the Natural History Museum more or less every second Sunday. I took the tram to Roslagstull and walked the rest of the way. The road was always a little longer than I had imagined. I remember those foot marches very clearly: it was always windy, my nose ran, my eyes filled with tears. I don't remember the journeys in the opposite direction. It's as if I never went home, only out to the museum, a sniffling, tearful, hopeful expedition toward a giant Babylonian building.

Finally arriving, I would be greeted by the elephant skeletons. I often went directly to the "old" part, the section with animals that had been stuffed back in the eighteenth century, some of them rather clumsily prepared, with swollen heads. Yet there was a special magic here. Big artificial landscapes with elegantly designed and positioned animal models failed to catch my interest—they were make-believe, something for children. No, it had to be quite clear that this was not a matter of living animals. They were stuffed, they stood there in the service of science. The scientific method I was closest to was the Linnean: discover, collect, examine.

I would work slowly through the museum. Long pauses among the whales and in the paleontology rooms. And then what detained me most: the invertebrates.

I never had any contact with other visitors. In fact, I don't remember other visitors being there at all. Other museums I occasionally visited—the National Maritime Museum, the National Museum of Ethnography, the Museum of Technology—were always crowded. But the Natural History Museum seemed to stay open only for me.

One day, however, I did encounter someone—no, not a visitor, he was a professor of some sort. We met among the invertebrates—he suddenly materialized between the display cases, and was almost as small in stature as I was. He spoke half to himself. At once we were involved in a discussion of molluscs. He was so absentminded or so unprejudiced that he treated me like an adult. One of those guardian angels who appeared now and then in my childhood and touched me with its wings.

Our conversation resulted in my being allowed into a section of the museum not open to the public. I was given much good advice on the preparation of small animals, and was equipped with little glass tubes that seemed to me truly professional.

I collected insects, above all beetles, from the age of eleven until I turned fifteen. Then other competing interests, mostly artistic, forced their attentions on me. How melancholy it felt that entomology must give way! I convinced myself that this was only a temporary adjustment. In fifty years or so I would resume my collecting.

My collecting would begin in the spring and then flourished of course in the summer, out on the island of Runmarö. In the summerhouse, where we had little enough space to move around, I kept jam jars with dead insects and a display board for butterflies. And lingering everywhere: the smell of ethyl acetate, a smell I carried with me since I always had a tin of this insect killer in my pocket.

It would no doubt have been more daring to use

potassium cyanide as the handbook recommended. Fortunately, this substance was not within my reach, so I never had to test my courage by choosing whether or not to use it.

Many were involved in the insect hunt. The neighborhood children learned to sound the alarm when they saw an insect that could be of interest. "Here's one!" echoed among the houses, and I would come rushing along with my butterfly net.

I went on endless expeditions. A life in the open air without the slightest thought of thereby improving my health. I had no aesthetic opinions on my booty, of course—this was, after all, Science—but I unknowingly absorbed many experiences of natural beauty. I moved in the great mystery. I learned that the ground was alive, that there was an infinite world of creeping and flying things living their own rich life without paying the least regard to us.

I caught a fraction of a fraction of that world and pinned it down in my boxes, which I still have. A hidden mini-museum of which I am seldom conscious. But they're sitting there, those insects. As if biding their time.

Primary School

I began in Katarina Norra Primary School and my teacher was Miss R., a tidy spinster who changed her clothes every day. When school ended each Saturday, each child was given a caramel, but otherwise she was strict. She was generous when it came to pulling hair and delivering blows, although she never hit me. I was the son of a teacher.

The first term, my chief task was to sit still at my desk. I could already write and count. I was allowed to sit and cut out shapes in colored paper, but what the shapes were I can't remember.

I have a feeling that the atmosphere was fairly good throughout my first year but that it chilled somewhat as time passed. Any disturbance to good order, any hitches or snags, made Miss R. lose her temper. We were not allowed to be restless or loud. We were not to whine. We were not to experience unexpected difficulties in learning something. Above all, we were not to do anything unexpected. Any little child who wet himself or herself in shame and fear could not hope for mercy.

As I said, being the son of a teacher saved me from blows. But I could feel the oppressive atmosphere generated by all those threats and reproaches. The head teacher was always in the background—hawk-nosed and dangerous. The very worst prospect was to be sent to a reform school, something which would be mentioned on special occasions. I never felt this as a threat to me personally, but the very idea caused a disagreeable sensation.

I could well imagine what a reformatory was like, the more so since I'd heard the name of one—Skrubba ("Scrub"), a name suggesting rasps and planes. I took it as self-evident that the inmates were subjected to daily torture. The world view that I had acquired allowed for the existence of special institutions where adults tortured children—perhaps to death—for having been noisy. A dreadful outlook. But so be it. If we were noisy, then ...

When a boy from our school was taken to a reformatory and then returned after a year, I regarded him as someone who had risen from the dead.

A more realistic threat was evacuation. During the first years of the war, plans were made for the evacuation of all schoolchildren from the bigger cities. Mother wrote the name TRANSTRÖMER with marking ink on our sheets, and so on. The question was whether I would be evacuated with mother and her school class or with my own class from Katarina Norra, i.e. deported with Miss R. I suspected the latter.

I escaped evacuation. Life at school went on. I spent all my time in school longing for the day to come to an end so that I could throw myself into what really interested me: Africa, the underwater world, the Middle Ages, etc. The only thing that really caught my attention in school was the wall charts. I was a devotee of wall charts. My greatest happiness was to accompany Miss R. to the storeroom to fetch some worn cardboard chart. While doing so I would peep at the other ones hanging inside. I tried to make some at home, as best I could.

One important difference between my life and that of my classmates was that I could not produce any father. The majority of my peers came from working-class families for whom divorce was clearly very rare. I would never admit that there was anything peculiar about my domestic situation. Not even to myself. No, of course I had a father, even if I saw him only once a year (usually on Christmas Eve). And I kept track of him—at one point during the war, for example, he was on a torpedo boat and sent me an amusing letter. I would have liked to have shared this letter in class but the opportunity never came up.

I remember a moment of panic. I had been absent for a couple of days, and when I came back a classmate told me that the teacher—not Miss R. but a substitute—had said to the class that they must not tease me on account of the fact that I had no father. In other words, they felt sorry for me. I panicked: I was obviously abnormal. I tried to talk it all away, my face bright red.

I was acutely aware of the danger of being regarded as an outsider because at heart I suspected I was one. I was absorbed in interests that no normal boy had. I joined a drawing class, voluntarily, and sketched underwater scenes: fish, sea urchins, crabs, shells. The teacher remarked out loud that my drawings were very "special" and my panic returned. There was a kind of insensitive adult who always wanted to point me out as somehow odd. My classmates were much more tolerant. I was neither popular nor bullied.

Hasse, a big darkish boy who was five times stronger than I was, had a habit of wrestling with me every break during our first year at school. In the beginning I resisted violently, but that got me nowhere for he just threw me to the ground and triumphed over me. At last I thought up a way of disappointing him: total relaxation. When he approached me I pretended that my Real Self had flown away leaving only a corpse behind, a lifeless rag that he could press to the ground as he wished. He soon lost interest.

I wonder what this method of turning myself into a lifeless rag has meant for me later on in life. The art of being ridden roughshod over while yet maintaining one's self-respect. Have I resorted to the trick too often? Sometimes it works, sometimes not.

The War

It was the spring of 1940. I was a skinny nine-year-old stooped over the newspaper, intent on the war map where black arrows indicated the advance of the German tank divisions. Those arrows penetrated France and for us, Hitler's enemies, they lived as parasites in our bodies. I really counted myself as one of Hitler's enemies. My political engagement has never been so wholehearted!

To write of the political engagement of a nine-year-old no doubt invites derision, but this was hardly a question of politics in the proper sense of the word. It meant simply that I took part in the war. I hadn't the slightest conception of matters such as social problems, classes, trade unions, the economy, the distribution of resources, the rival claims of socialism and capitalism. A "Communist" was someone who supported Russia. "Right wing" was a shady term since those at that end of the political spectrum often had German leanings. And were understood to be rich. Yet what did it really mean to be rich? On a few occasions we were invited for a meal with a family who were described as rich. They lived in Äppelviken and the master of the house was a wholesale dealer. A large villa, servants in black and white. I noticed that the boy in the family—he was my age—had an incredibly big toy car, a fire engine, highly desirable. How did one get hold of such a thing? I had a momentary glimpse of the idea that the family belonged to a different social class, one in which people could afford unusually large toy cars. This is still an isolated and not very important memory.

Another memory: during a visit to a classmate's home, I was surprised there was no toilet, only a dry closet out in the backyard, like the kind we had in the country. We would pee into a discarded saucepan which my friend's mother would swill down the kitchen sink. It was picturesque detail. On the whole it didn't occur to me that the family lacked this or that. And the villa in Äppelviken did not strike me as remarkable. I was far short of the capacity that many seem to have acquired, even in their early years, of grasping the class status and economic level of a given environment merely at a glance. Many children seemed able to do so, not I.

My "political" instincts were directed entirely at the war and Nazism. I believed one was either a Nazi or an anti-Nazi. I had no understanding of that lukewarm attitude, that opportunistic wait-and-see stance which was widespread in Sweden. I interpreted this either as support for the Allies or as covert Nazism. When I realized some person I liked was really "pro-German," I immediately felt a terrible tightening over my breast. Everything was ruined. There could never be any kind of fellow feeling between us.

From those close to me I expected unequivocal support. One evening when we were on a visit to Uncle Elof and Aunt Agda, the news inspired my generally taciturn uncle to comment that "the English are successfully retreating …" He said this with slight regret mixed with an ironic undertone (on the whole irony was foreign to him) and I suddenly felt that terrible tightening. The Allied version of history was never questioned. I stared grimly up at the roof light for consolation. It had the shape of a British steel helmet: like a soup plate.

On Sundays we often had dinner in Enskede with my other uncle and aunt on Mother's side; they provided a sort of surrogate family for Mother after the divorce. It was part of their ritual to turn on the BBC's Swedish radio broadcast. I shall never forget the program's opening flourish: first the victory signal and then the signature tune, which was alleged to be Purcell's *Trumpet Voluntary* but which in fact was a rather puffed-up arrangement of a harpsichord piece by Jeremiah Clarke. The announcer's calm voice, with a shade of an accent, spoke directly to me from a world of friendly heroes who saw to it that it was business as usual even if bombs were raining down.

When we were on the suburban train on the way to Enskede I always wanted Mother—who hated attracting attention—to unfold the propaganda paper *News from Great Britain,* and thus silently make public our stance. She did nearly everything for me, including that.

I seldom met Father during the war. But one day he popped up and took me to a party with his journalist friends. The glasses were standing ready, there were voices and laughter, and the cigarette smoke was dense. I was led around, being introduced and answering questions. The atmosphere was relaxed and tolerant and I could do what I wanted. I withdrew by myself and sidled along the bookshelves of this strange house.

I came across a newly published book called *The Martyrdom of Poland.* Documentary. I settled on the floor and read it from cover to cover while the voices filled the air. That terrible book—which I have never seen again—contained what I feared, or perhaps what I hoped for. The Nazis were as inhuman as I had imagined—no, they were worse! I read fascinated and disturbed, and at the same time a feeling of triumph emerged: I'd been right! It was all in the book, detailed proof! Just wait! One day everything will be revealed; one day all of you who have doubted will have the truth thrown in your faces. Just wait! And that, in the event, is what happened.

Libraries

Medborgarhuset (The Citizens' House) was built around 1940. A big four-square block in the middle of Söder, but also a bright and promising edifice, modern, "functional." It was only five minutes from where we lived.

It contained, among other things, a public swimming pool and a branch of the city library. The children's section was, by obvious natural necessity, my allotted sphere, and in the beginning had enough books for my consumption. The most important was Brehm's *Lives of the Animals*.

I slipped into the library nearly every day. But this was not an entirely trouble-free process. It sometimes happened that I tried to borrow books that the library ladies did not consider suitable for my age. One was Knut Holmboe's violent documentary *The Desert Is Burning*.

"Who is to have this book?"

"I am …"

"Oh no …"

"I …"

"You can tell your father he can come and borrow it himself."

It was even worse when I tried to get into the adult section. I needed a book that was definitely not in the children's section. I was stopped at the entrance.

"How old are you?"

"Eleven."

"You can't borrow books here. You can come back in a few years."

"Yes, but the book I want is only in here."

"What book?"

"The Animals of Scandinavia: A History of Their Migration." And I added, "by Ekman," in hollow tones, feeling the game was lost. It was. Out of the question. I blushed, I was furious. I would never forgive her!

In the meantime my uncle of few words—Uncle Elof—intervened. He gave me his card to the adult section and we maintained the fiction that I was collecting books for him. I could now get in where I wanted.

The adult section shared a wall with the pool. At the entrance one felt the fumes from within, the chlorine smell drifted through the ventilation system and the echoing voices could be heard as from a distance.

Swimming pools and suchlike always have strange acoustics. The temple of health and the temple of books were neighbors—a good idea. I was a faithful visitor to the Medborgarhus branch of the city library for many years. I regarded it as clearly superior to the central library up on Sveavägen—where the atmosphere was heavier and the air was still, no fumes of chlorine, no echoing voices. The books themselves had a different smell there; it gave me headaches.

Once given free rein of the library I devoted my attention mostly to nonfiction. I left literature to its fate. Likewise the shelves marked Economics and Social Problems. History, though, was interesting. Medicine scared me.

But it was Geography that was my favorite corner. I was a special devotee of the Africa shelves, which were extensive. I can recall titles like *Mount Elgon, A Market-Boy in Africa, Desert Sketches* … I wonder if any of those books still fill the shelves.

Someone called Albert Schweitzer had written a book enticingly called *Between Water and Primeval Forest*. It consisted mostly of speculations about life. But Schweitzer himself stayed put in his mission and

didn't move; he wasn't a proper explorer. Not like, for
instance, Gösta Moberg, who covered endless miles
(why?) in alluring, unknown regions, such as Niger
or Chad, lands about which there was scant information in the library. Kenya and Tanganyika, however,
were favored on account of their Swedish settlements.
Tourists who sailed up the Nile to the Sudd area and
then turned north again—they wrote books. But not
those who ventured into the arid zones of the Sudan,
nor those who made their way into Kordofan or Dar-
fur. The Portuguese colonies of Angola and Mozam-
bique, which looked so big on the map, were also
unknown and neglected areas on the Africa shelves,
making them even more attractive.

I read a lot of books while in the library—I didn't
want to take home too many books of the same kind,
or the same book several times in succession. I felt I
would be criticized by the library staff and that was
something to be avoided at all costs.

One summer—I don't remember which one—I
lived through an elaborate and persistent daydream
about Africa. I was on the island of Runmarö, a long
way from the library. I withdrew into a fantasy and

was leading an expedition straight through central Africa. I trudged on through the woods of Runmarö and kept track of roughly how far I'd gone with a dotted line on a big map of Africa, a map of the whole continent that I had drawn. If I worked out, for instance, that in the course of a week I had walked 120 kilometers on Runmarö, I marked 120 kilometers on the map. Not very far.

At first I'd thought of starting the expedition on the east coast, more or less where Stanley had begun. But that would have left too great a distance to traverse before I could reach the most interesting parts. I changed my mind and imagined that I traveled as far as Albert Nyansa by car. And this was where the expedition proper started, on foot. I would then have at least a reasonable chance of putting most of the Ituri Forest behind me before summer ended.

It was a nineteenth-century expedition, with bearers, etc. I was half aware, though, that this was now an obsolete way of traveling. Africa had changed. There was war in British Somaliland; it was in the news. Tanks were in action. Indeed, it was the first area where the Allies could claim an advance—I took due note of this, of course—and Abyssinia was the first country to be liberated from the Axis powers.

When my Africa dream returned several years later, it became modernized and was now almost realistic. I was thinking of becoming an entomologist and collecting insects in Africa, discovering new species instead of new deserts.

Grammar School

Only a couple of my classmates from primary school progressed to secondary school (*realskola*). And no one apart from myself applied to Södra Latin Grammar School.

There was an entrance exam I had to pass. My sole memory of this is spelling the word *särskilt* (especially) wrong: I gave it two ls. From then on the word had a disturbing effect on me which persisted far into the 1960s.

I have a distinct memory of my first day at Södra Latin in the autumn of 1942. It is as follows: I find myself surrounded by a number of unfamiliar eleven-year-old boys. I have butterflies in my stomach; I'm uncertain and alone. But some of the others seem to know each other well—these are the pupils from Maria Preparatory. I look and look for a face from Katarina Norra. My mood consists of equal parts gloomy unease and hopeful expectation.

Our names are called out and we are divided into three classes. I am assigned to Class 15B and told to follow Dr. Mohlin, who is to be our teacher. He's one of the oldest teachers; his subject is German. He is small, with a sort of catlike authority, and moves swiftly and quietly; he has bristly, reluctantly greying hair, and a bald wedge above each temple. From someone nearby who seems to know him, I catch an assessment of him: Målle—as he is called—is "strict but fair." Ominous.

From the first moment it was clear that grammar school was something quite different from primary school. Södra Latin was thoroughly masculine, the school was as single-sexed as a monastery or barracks. It was not until several years later that a couple of women were smuggled onto the staff.

Each morning we all assembled in the school hall, sang hymns, and listened to a sermon delivered by one of the religious studies teachers. Then we marched off to our respective classrooms. The collective atmosphere of Södra Latin was immortalized by Ingmar Bergman in his film *Hets*.* (It was shot in the school and those of us who were pupils appeared as extras in several scenes of the film.)

We were all supplied with a school manual that in-

* In Britain the film was called *Frenzy*, and in the USA, *Torment*.

cluded, among other items, "Directives as to order and discipline, in accordance with the school's statutes":

> The pupils shall attend instruction at the determined times, neatly and decently attired and in possession of the necessary textbooks. They shall observe good order and proper conduct and shall follow the instruction with due attention. The pupils shall likewise attend morning devotions and there deport themselves quietly and attentively....
>
> Pupils shall give due respect and obedience to the staff of the institution and shall accept with compliance their commands, corrections, and chastisements....

Södra Latin occupied the highest site on Söder, and its playground formed a plateau above most of the district's rooftops. The bricks of the school building could be seen from far away. The route to this castle of sighs was one I generally completed at a half-run. I hurried along by the long piles of wood—a sign of the crisis years—in front of "Björns Trädgård," made my way up Götgatan—past Hansson and Bruce's bookshop—swung to the left into Höbergsgatan where, every winter morning, a horse stood chewing straw from a nosebag. It was a brewery horse, a big steaming Ardenne. For a moment I found myself in its reeking shadow. I still have a vivid memory of this patient beast, its smell in the cold and damp. A smell that was at once suffocating and comforting.

I would rush into the playground just as the bells began to summon us to morning service. I was hardly ever late, for everything between the hours of eight and nine in the morning was well-timed. The spring was firm and tense as the school day began.

The end of the day at school was, of course, more relaxed, less regulated. Sometimes I went home with Palle. He was my closest friend during my first year at Södra Latin. We had quite a lot in common: his father, a sailor, was absent for long periods, and he was the only child of a good-natured mother who seemed pleased to see me. Palle had developed many of the characteristics of a single child, as I had, and he lived for his interests. He was above all a collector. Of what? Anything. Beer labels, matchboxes, swords, flint axes, stamps, postcards, shells, ethnographic oddities, and bones.

In his home, which was crammed full of his booty,

we would duel with the swords. Together we carried out excavations at a secret spot on Riddarholmen and managed to retrieve bits of skeleton, which my dentist identified as "parts of a human being."

Having Palle as a friend was an enriching experience, but we gradually drifted apart. Further on in school Palle was absent for long stretches because of illness. When he was transferred to another class we lost touch. My old friend was very far away. In fact, he was marked by death. He appeared at school now only occasionally, pale and serious, with one leg amputated. When he died I found it impossible to accept. I developed a bad conscience but refused to recognize it. I felt as if I was supposed to suppress the memory of all the fun we'd had.

I feel I'm the same age as Palle, who died forty-five years ago without having grown up. But my old teachers, the "oldies" as they were collectively termed, remain old in my memory despite the fact that the older among them were about the same age as I am now as I write this. We always feel younger than we are. I carry inside myself my earlier faces, as a tree contains its rings. The sum of them is "me." The mirror sees only my latest face, while I know all my previous ones.

The teachers who stand out in my memory are, of course, those who generated tension or excitement, those who were vivid, colorful, original. They were not in the majority but there were a fair number of them. We were able to sense something tragic about some of them. A critical situation that could be described thus: "I know I can't be loved by those enviable turnipheads in front of me. I know I can't be loved, but at least I can make sure I won't be forgotten!"

The classroom was a theater. The leading player, the teacher, performed on the stage, subjected to merciless scrutiny. The pupils were the audience and sometimes—one at a time—they would act a part as well.

We had to be on our guard, unfailingly. I had to get used to the recurring outbursts of aggression. Miss R. had laid a good foundation—she had been strict and heavy-handed. Yet not really theatrical. At home there was nothing like this for me to learn—no scenes, no rows, no bellowing father figure. Mother was spontaneous but undramatic. Giving vent to anger was childish. I had often been furious as a child but now I was a reasonably balanced youngster. My ideals were

English—a stiff upper lip and so on. Outbursts of rage belonged to the Axis Powers.

At school there were choleric prima donnas who could devote most of a lesson to building up a tower of hysterical indignation with the sole purpose of then emptying their vessels of wrath.

My class teacher, Målle, was hardly a prima donna. But he was the victim of a periodic and irresistible fury. Målle was really a charming person and a good teacher in his more harmonious periods. But, unhappily, what I remember most is his fury. Possibly the more violent outbursts did not come more often than three or four times a month. But it was upon those occasions that his great authority undoubtedly rested.

In the course of such lessons the thunder rolled back and forth across the landscape. That lightning would strike was clear to everyone, but no one could predict where. Målle did not victimize certain pupils. He was "strict but fair." Anyone might be struck by lightning.

One day lightning struck me. We were told to open our German grammars. I couldn't find mine. Was it in my schoolbag? Forgotten at home? I was lost. I couldn't find it.

"Stand up!"

I saw Målle dance down from his desk and close in on me. It was like being out in a field watching a bull approach.

The cuffs rained down on me. I staggered this way and that. The next moment Målle was back sitting at his desk, frothing with rage, writing out a note for home. It was worded rather vaguely, accusing me of having been "careless during a lesson" or something.

Many of the teachers hoped those written notes home would lead to interrogations and the infliction of further punishments at the hands of parents.

Not so with me. Mother listened to my story, took the note, and signed it. She then noticed that I had blue marks on my face, caused by the ringed hand of the pedagogue. Her reaction was unexpectedly strong. She said she would contact the school, perhaps phone the headmaster.

I protested. She couldn't do that! Everything had turned out OK. But now "scandal" threatened. I would be called a "mama's boy" and then persecuted forever, not just by Målle but by the entire staff.

She dropped the idea of course. And throughout

my school days I made a point of keeping the two worlds—school and home—apart. If the two worlds were to seep into each other, then home would feel polluted. I would no longer have any proper refuge. Even today I find something disagreeable in the phrase "cooperation between home and school." I can also see that this holding apart of the separate worlds that I practiced gave rise in due course to a more deliberately maintained distinction between private life and society. (This has nothing to do with political inclinations, whether to the left or to the right.) What we live through in school is projected as an image of society. My total experience of school was mixed, with more darkness than light—just as my image of society has become. (Although we could well ask what we mean by "society.")

Contact between teacher and pupil was intensely personal, and important personal characteristics were magnified in the classroom atmosphere as the result of the many tense situations. Personal, yes, but not in the slightest private. We knew virtually nothing about the private life of our teachers although most of them lived in the streets around the school. There were, naturally, rumors—like Målle having been a feather-weight boxer in his youth—but they were feebly supported by proper evidence and we scarcely gave them credit. We had trustworthy information about two of the most discreet younger teachers, men who never inspired any drama. One of them was poor and eked out his salary by playing the piano at a restaurant in the evening. He was seen. The other was a chess champion. He was in the newspaper.

One day in autumn Målle came into a lesson with a *Russula aerugina* in his hand. He set the mushroom on his desk. It was both liberating and shocking to have caught a glimpse of his private life! We now knew Målle gathered mushrooms.

None of the teachers expressed political opinions. But at that time there were of course unprecedented tensions in the staff room. The Second World War was being fought here, too. Many of the teachers were committed Nazis. As late as 1944 one of them, it was said, exclaimed in the staff room, "If Hitler falls, then *I* shall fall!" He didn't fall, however. I had him in German later. He recovered so well that he was able to welcome Hesse's Nobel Prize in 1946 with triumphant bellowing.

I was a worthy pupil but not one of the best. Biology ought to have been my favorite subject, but for most of my secondary schooling I had a peculiar biology teacher. At some point in the past he had hopelessly blotted his copybook; he was warned and was now like a quenched volcano. My best subjects were geography and history. An assistant teacher called Brännman taught these classes. Ruddy and energetic, Brännman was a youngish man whose straight blond hair had a tendency to stand on end when he got angry, which happened quite often. He had plenty of goodwill and I liked him. The essays I wrote were always on geographical or historical subjects. They were long. Regarding this, I heard a story much later from another Södra Latin pupil, Bo Grandien.* Bo became a close friend of mine in the later years of school but what he told me related to an earlier year when we didn't know each other.

He said the first time he heard my name mentioned was as he passed some of my classmates during a break. They had just been given back their essays and were dissatisfied with their grades. Bo heard the indignant

---

* The poet and journalist (b. 1932).

remark: "We can't *all* write as fast as Tranan, can we?" *

Bo decided that "Tranan" was a detestable character who ought to be avoided. To me, this story is in a way comforting. Nowadays, well-known for deficient productivity, I was then clearly noted as a prolific scribbler, someone who sinned through excessive productivity, a literal Stakhanov.

* "Tranan": the crane (the bird).

Exorcism

During the winter when I was fifteen I was afflicted by a severe form of anxiety. I was trapped by a searchlight that radiated not light but darkness. I was caught each afternoon as twilight fell and not released from its terrible grip until the next day dawned. I slept very little; I sat up in bed, usually with a thick book before me. I read several thick books during this time but I can't say I really read them, for they left no trace in my memory. The books were a pretext for leaving the light on.

It began in late autumn. One evening I'd gone to the cinema and seen *Squandered Days*, a film about an alcoholic. It ends with him in a state of delirium—a harrowing sequence that today I would perhaps find rather childish. But not then.

As I lay down to sleep I reran the film in my mind's eye, as one does after being at the cinema.

Suddenly the atmosphere in the room was tense with dread. Something took total possession of me. Suddenly my body started shaking, especially my legs. I was a clockwork toy that had been wound up and now rattled and jumped helplessly. The cramps were quite beyond the control of my will—I had never experienced anything like this. I screamed for help and Mother appeared. Gradually the cramps ebbed away. And did not return. But my dread intensified and from dusk to dawn would not leave me alone. The feeling that dominated my nights was the terror Fritz Lang nearly captured in certain scenes of *The Testament of Dr. Mabuse*, especially the opening scene: a factory where someone hides while the machines and room vibrate. I recognized myself in this immediately, although my nights were quieter.

The most important element in my existence was *illness*. The world was a vast hospital. I saw before me human beings deformed in body and in soul. The light burned and tried to hold back the terrible faces but sometimes I would doze off, my eyelids would close, and the terrible faces would suddenly close in on me.

It all happened in silence, yet within the silence voices were endlessly busy. The wallpaper pattern made faces. Now and then the silence would be broken by a ticking in the walls. Produced by what? By whom? By me? The walls crackled because my sick thoughts wanted them to. So much the worse … Was I insane? Almost.

I was afraid of drifting into madness but in general I did not feel threatened by any kind of illness—it was scarcely a case of hypochondria—but it was rather the total power of illness that aroused terror. As in a film where an innocuous apartment interior changes its character entirely when ominous music is heard, I now experienced the outer world quite differently because it included my awareness of the domination wielded by sickness. A few years previously I had wanted to be an explorer. Now I had pushed my way into an unknown country where I had never wanted to be. I had discovered an evil power. Or rather, the evil power had discovered me.

I read recently about some teenagers who lost all their joy in living because they became obsessed with the idea that AIDS had taken over the world. They would have understood me.

Mother had witnessed the cramps I suffered that evening in late autumn as my crisis began. But then she could only be an outsider. Everyone had to be excluded; what was going on was just too terrible to be discussed. I was surrounded by ghosts. I myself was a ghost. A ghost who walked to school every morning and sat through the lessons without revealing its secret. School had become a breathing space, my dread wasn't the same there. It was my private life that was haunted. Everything was upside down.

At that time I was skeptical of all forms of religion and I certainly said no prayers. If the crisis had arisen a few years later I would have been able to experience it as a revelation, something that would rouse me, like Siddhartha's four encounters (with an old person, with a sick person, with a corpse, and with a begging monk). I would have managed to feel a little more sympathy for, and a little less dread of, the deformed and the sick who invaded my nocturnal consciousness. But back then, caught in my dread, religiously colored explanations were not available to me. No prayers, but attempts at exorcism by way of music. I began to hammer at the piano in earnest.

And all the time I was growing. At the beginning of the autumn term I was one of the smallest in the class, but by its end I was one of the tallest. As if the dread I lived in were a kind of fertilizer helping the plant shoot up.

Winter moved toward its end and the days length-
ened. Now, miraculously, the darkness in my own
life withdrew. It happened gradually and I was slow
in fully realizing what was happening. One spring
evening I discovered that all my terrors were now
marginal. I sat with some friends philosophizing and
smoking cigars. It was time to walk home through the
pale spring night and I had no dread at all of terrors
waiting for me at home.

Still, it is something I have taken part in. Possibly
my most important experience. But it came to an end.
I thought it was the Inferno but it was Purgatory.

Latin

In the autumn of 1946 I entered the Latin division of senior secondary school (upper high school). This meant new teachers: instead of Målle, Satan, Slöman (*slö* = dull), and company came characters like Fjalar, Fido, Lillan (the littl'un), Moster (Auntie), and Bocken (The Buck). The last of these was the most important because he was my class teacher and influenced me more than I would have been willing to admit then as our personalities clashed.

A few years before he became my teacher, we had had a moment of dramatic contact. I was late one day and was running along one of the school corridors. Another boy came hurtling in the opposite direction toward me. This was G., who belonged to a parallel class and was well known as a bully. We screeched to a halt, face-to-face, without quite managing to avoid a collision. This sudden braking generated a lot of aggression and we were alone in the corridor. G. took the chance offered—his right fist slammed into my midriff. My sight blackened and I fell to the floor, moaning like a mademoiselle in a nineteenth-century novel. G. vanished.

As the darkness cleared I found myself staring up at a figure stooping over me. A drawn-out, whining, singing voice kept repeating as if in despair, "What's the matter? What's the matter?" I saw a pink face and very neatly trimmed chalk-white beard. The expression on the face was worried.

That voice, that face, belonged to the Latin and Greek teacher Per Venström, alias Pelle Vänster (*vänster* = left), alias Bocken. Fortunately he refrained from any kind of interrogation as to why I was lying in a heap on the floor, and he seemed satisfied when he saw I could walk away unaided. Since he showed himself to be worried and somewhat helpful, I formed the impression that Bocken was at heart a well-meaning person. Something of that impression persisted later as well, even when we had our conflicts.

Bocken's appearance was stylish, quite theatrical indeed. He usually accompanied his white beard with a dark wide-brimmed hat and a short cloak. A minimum of outdoor clothes in winter. An obvious touch of Dracula. At a distance he was superior and decorative, close up his face often conveyed a helplessness.

The half-singing intonation that characterized him was a personal elaboration of the Gotland dialect.

Bocken suffered from a chronic arthritic condition and had an emphatic limp, yet he managed to move swiftly. He always made a dramatic entrance into the classroom, throwing his briefcase onto his desk; then, after a few seconds, we knew without a doubt whether his mood was favorable or stormy. The state of the weather evidently affected his mood. On cool days his lessons could be downright jovial. When an area of low pressure hovered over us and the skies were cloudy, his lessons crawled along in a dull and fretful atmosphere punctuated by those inescapable outbursts of rage.

He belonged to the category of human being that was quite impossible to imagine in a role other than that of schoolteacher. In fact, it could be said that it was hard to envisage him as anything other than a Latin teacher.

In the course of my penultimate year at school, my own brand of modernistic poetry was in production. At the same time I was drawn to older poetry, and when our Latin lessons moved forward from the his-

torical texts on wars, senators, and consuls to verses by
Catullus and Horace, I was carried quite willingly into
the poetic world presided over by Bocken.

Plodding through verses was educative. It went like
this. The pupils first had to read out a stanza, from
Horace perhaps:

> Aequam memento rebus in arduis
> servare mentem, non secus in bonis
>   ab insolenti temperatam
>   laetitia, morituri Delli

Bocken would cry out: "Translate!" And the pupil
would oblige:

> With an even temper … aah … Remember that
> in an even temper … no … with equanimity … to
> maintain an even temper in difficult conditions,
> and not otherwise … aah … and like in fav- … fa-
> vorable conditions … aah … abstain from exces-
> sive … aah … vivacious joy O mortal Dellius …

By now the luminous Roman text had really been
brought down to earth. But in the next moment, in
the next stanza, Horace came back in Latin with the

miraculous precision of his verse. This alternation between the trivial and decrepit on the one hand and the buoyant and sublime on the other taught me a lot. It had to do with the conditions of poetry and of life. That through form something could be raised to another level. The caterpillar feet were gone, the wings unfolded. One should never lose hope!

Alas, Bocken never realized how captivated I was by those classical stanzas. To him I was a quietly provocative schoolboy whose incomprehensible nineteen-fortyish poems appeared in the school magazine—that was in the autumn of 1948. When he saw my efforts, with their consistent avoidance of capitals and punctuation marks, he reacted with indignation. I was to be identified as part of the advancing tide of barbarism. Such a person must be utterly immune to Horace.

His image of me was further tarnished after a medieval Latin lesson dealing with life in the thirteenth century. It was an overcast day; Bocken was in pain, and his rage was just waiting to explode. Suddenly he tossed out the question: who was "Erik the Lame Lisper"? Erik had been referred to in our text. I replied that he was the founder of Grönköping.* This was a reflex action on my part stemming from my wish to lighten the oppressive atmosphere. But Bocken was angry, not simply then and there but even at the end of term when I was given a "warning." This was a brief written message home to the effect that the pupil had been negligent in the subject, in this case Latin. Since my grades for written work were all high, this "warning" presumably referred to life in general rather than to my performance in Latin.

In my last year at school our relationship improved. By the time I took my exams it was quite cordial.

Around then two Horatian stanza forms, the sapphic and the alcaic, began to find their way into my own writing. In the summer after matriculation I wrote two poems in sapphic stanzas. The one was "Ode to Thoreau," later pruned down to "Five Stanzas to Thoreau," the more juvenile parts having been erased. The other was "Storm," in the sequence "Autumnal Archipelago." But I don't know if Bocken ever

---

* The archetypal small town. According to the satirical weekly *Grönköpings Veckoblad* the town was founded by King Erik Eriksson (1216–1250), known as Erik the Lame Lisper.

acquainted himself with these. Classical meters—how did I come to use them? The idea simply turned up. For I regarded Horace as a contemporary. He was like René Char, Oskar Loerke, or Einar Malm. The idea was so naïve it became sophisticated.

Memories Look at Me

A June morning, too soon to wake,
too late to fall asleep again.

I must go out—the greenery is dense
with memories, they follow me with their gaze.

They can't be seen, they merge completely into
the background, true chameleons.

They are so close that I can hear them breathe
though the birdsong is deafening.